WEIRD AND WONDERFUL SNAKES

MIKE LINLEY

Thomson Learning
New York

WEIRD AND WONDERFUL

FISH
FROGS & TOADS
INSECTS
SNAKES

Cover: An eyelash viper from Costa Rica.

First published in the United States in 1993 by
Thomson Learning, 115 Fifth Avenue, New York, NY 10003

First published in 1991 by Wayland (Publishers) Limited
61 Western Road, Hove, East Sussex BN3 1JD, England

Library of Congress Cataloging-in-Publication Data

Linley, Mike.
Snakes / Mike Linley.
p. cm.—(Weird and wonderful)
Originally published: Hove, East Sussex, England : Wayland, 1991.
Includes bibliographical references and index.
Summary: Describes the characteristics of several species of snakes considered unique and distinct because of their physiology, habits, and habitats.
ISBN 1-56847-006-1
1. Snakes—Juvenile literature. [1. Snakes.] I. Title. II. Series.
QL666.O6L728 1993
597.96—dc20 91-8558

Printed in the United States of America

CONTENTS

1. Biggest and smallest

There are between 2,500 and 3,000 different types of snakes found nearly all over the world. Although snakes are all much the same, they do vary enormously in size. The reticulated python is undoubtedly the world's largest. It can reach a length of 33 ft (10 m). It lives all over Southeast Asia where it feeds on deer and wild pigs.

Although the anaconda does not quite reach the same length as the python, it can take the title of the world's heaviest snake. It can weigh up to 440 lb (200 kg), and its body is so thick and heavy that it has to spend most of its time in water. The anaconda lives in the rivers of **tropical** South America. It lies in wait for large animals that go down to the water's edge for a drink.

The world's smallest snake is the tiny thread, or bootlace, snake from islands in the Caribbean. It rarely reaches even 6 in (15 cm) in length and is hardly thicker than the lead in a pencil.

Below This bird is just a snack for the huge reticulated python.

Right This picture shows how thick and heavy the anaconda's body is.

2. On the move

Snakes move in a variety of ways. Most slither from side to side, pushing their bodies against obstacles to drive themselves forward. The coachwhip snake from North America can move this way faster than a person can walk. Other snakes glide along in a straight line, raising segments of the body off the ground to move forward.

Perhaps the most interesting way a snake moves is the motion of the sidewinders. These snakes live in the hot deserts of the southwestern United States. They have to move at high speed over the loose, scorching sand. Any other snake would wiggle hopelessly from side to side without getting anywhere and would soon be eaten by **predators.** The sidewinder coils up in the form of an "S" and then throws its body sideways, "skipping" over the sand. As the snake moves this way, only small parts of its underside touch the sand at any one time. This is just as well, since the sand is so hot.

Left The sidewinder leaves distinctive tracks in the sand as it travels.

Below Coachwhip snakes slither very quickly along the ground.

3. Acrobats and burrowers

Many snakes live in trees where they hunt for birds and small **reptiles.** One type of snake has developed a really strange way of escaping from predators. The flying snake, from Southeast Asia, lives high up in the treetops, often 100 ft (30 m) from the ground. If it sees a predator such as a hawk approaching, it leaps out of the tree and into the air. It does not actually fly—no reptile can do that—but it can change its shape so that it becomes flatter and its body acts like a **parachute.** The snake rarely falls all the way to the ground but usually lands among the branches of a nearby tree. Flying snakes can reach a length of about 5 ft (1.5 m).

While some snakes spend their time high up in the treetops, others live entirely underground. The African burrowing snake appears above ground only when heavy rains flood its burrow. It is able to move its thin, smooth body just as easily backward as it can move it forward while it hunts its **prey** in the total darkness.

Below This flying snake can leap from treetops.

Right The burrowing snake lives and hunts underground.

4. In and out of water

Almost all snakes are able to swim, especially when they have to escape danger or catch **aquatic** animals for food. Sea snakes spend their entire lives at sea. They are found in the warmer parts of the Indian and Pacific oceans and in some smaller hot, tropical seas. The sea snake's body is flattened from side to side to help it swim through the water. Some types only come ashore to lay their eggs under stones on a beach. Others, such as the **pelagic** sea snake, give birth to live, fully-formed young in the ocean, so they never leave the sea. Sea snakes feed on fish and are among the most **venomous** of snakes.

By contrast, the horned viper may never even see a drop of water. It lives in the Sahara in North Africa and spends most of its time lying in wait for prey, its body hidden from view just beneath the sand. The horned viper gets almost all the water it needs from the mammals and reptiles that it feeds on.

Left The North African horned viper rarely sees a drop of water.

Below The venomous sea snake can be dangerous. Divers beware!

5. Eaten: dead or alive

Snakes use a variety of methods to eat their prey. Many snakes kill their prey by **constriction.** The boa constrictor is a good example. It reaches a length of about 13 ft (4 m) and feeds on small animals up to about the size of a small dog. Once it has seized its prey in its jaws, the boa throws its body around it in tight coils. But it does not crush its victim as many people think. Instead, the boa suffocates it by tightening its grip slowly but firmly. This prevents the animal from breathing. Once the prey has died and is no longer moving, the boa releases its grip and uncoils its body. It then finds the head end of its prey and starts to swallow it.

Not all snakes kill their prey before swallowing it. The European grass snake, for example, swallows small animals, such as frogs, newts, and fish, alive. The animal suffocates after a few minutes of being trapped inside the snake's body. The prey can then be digested.

Below Grass snakes swallow their prey while it is still alive.

Right The strong boa constrictor kills by suffocation.

6. Finding a meal

Snakes hunt their prey in many different ways. Some hide and wait for animals to come within range of their **strike.** Others find their prey using a combination of sight and **scent.**

The pit viper has another way of detecting food. It feeds on warm-blooded mammals and birds and has special heat-detecting organs in its head. These "pit" organs lie between the nostrils and the eyes and look like an extra pair of large nostrils. They are very sensitive and can sense the heat of an animal's body standing out against the cooler air around it. The snake can thus detect and track down prey in complete darkness. Pit vipers are extremely venomous.

Instead of seeking out its prey, the Australian death adder lies in wait for prey and can actually attract animals toward it. It does this by wriggling its brightly colored tail, which looks like a large tasty worm. Any lizard that is attracted to the "worm" is quickly seized and eaten.

Left The pit viper can detect the body heat of other animals.

Below This death adder is trying to attract prey to its mouth.

7. Defensive displays

Rattlesnakes have a very bad reputation. Anyone who has seen a "Western" movie will know that. But like all snakes, rattlers are shy creatures and would rather avoid coming into contact with people or other large animals. The rattlesnake has a rattle made up of old scales, left after the snake has shed its skin a number of times, that fit loosely over one another. When a rattlesnake is threatened or is angry, as when an intruder approaches, it shakes its rattle. The buzzing sound warns intruders of the rattlesnake's presence, and to keep away.

The many species of cobra that live in Africa and Asia are also quick to warn intruders of their presence. When disturbed, they rear up and flatten out the loose skin in the neck region to form a **hood.** This makes their heads look three or four times their actual size. Some cobras have large eye spots on their hoods to startle intruders even more.

Below As a last resort, a rattle-snake will strike if threatened.

Right This Indian cobra makes an impressive display when threatened.

8. Dangerous and harmless

Venomous snakes, including cobras, rattlesnakes, and coral snakes, use venom to kill prey and for self-defense. Most venomous snakes have hollow **fangs** with an opening at the point, like a hypodermic needle. The venom trickles down inside the tooth and into the wound the snake makes when it bites.

One type of cobra, the spitting cobra, has different fangs so that it can spit out venom. The opening of the fang is halfway down the front of the tooth. The snake can squirt the venom straight forward into its victim's face. It is able to spit its venom very accurately over a distance of about 6½ ft (2 m). The spitting cobra aims mainly at the eyes of its victim and, if it hits its target, the venom can cause acute pain and even blindness.

In contrast to the aggressive spitting cobra, the North American hognose snake avoids having to defend itself altogether. If threatened, the harmless hognose snake simply rolls over onto its back, opens its mouth and pretends to be dead. Most predators then lose interest and leave it alone. After a few minutes, the snake rights itself and slithers away.

Left This spitting cobra is getting ready to aim its venom.

Below The hognose snake is very convincing when playing dead.

9. Watch out!

Many types of venomous snakes warn other animals that they are dangerous and likely to bite if attacked.

The coral snake shows that it is dangerous by being very brightly colored. It has bands of bright red and yellow as well as black around its body. Red and yellow are common warning colors in the animal kingdom. Most animals seeing the snake will recognize the colors and leave it alone.

Some nonvenomous snakes take advantage of this type of defense. The scarlet king snake, for example, lives in the same area as the coral snake and has almost the same coloration. An animal that sees a scarlet king snake might mistake it for a dangerous coral snake and leave it alone.

Below Most animals try to avoid the deadly coral snake.

Right The harmless scarlet king snake mimics the coral snake.

10. Open wide...

Some snakes will eat almost any animal they come across. Others are very choosy about the prey they eat. For example, some will eat only frogs, others earthworms; others lizards.

There is one type of snake in Africa that eats only birds' eggs. Not surprisingly, this snake is called the egg-eating snake. The snake grows to a little over 3 ft (about 1 m), and its body is about the thickness of a human finger. However, it can easily swallow a hen's egg whole—without even breaking the shell.

The snake can do this because it, like other snakes, is able to unhinge its jaw and spread its very elastic mouth wide open. It takes the egg in its mouth and swallows it. Then, a special row of rough teeth inside the snake's throat rub against the egg and break the shell. The contents of the egg pass into the snake's stomach, and the snake can then spit out the broken eggshell. This way none of the egg is spilled.

Left The egg-eating snake loosens its jaws to stretch over the egg.

Below Once inside the snake's throat, the egg is broken up.

11. Hidden danger

To avoid enemies, many snakes rely on camouflage. This means they are colored and patterned in a way that makes them match their background.

One type of eyelash viper lives in the moss-covered trees of the tropical rainforests of Central America. Its green pattern means not only that it cannot be seen by its enemies but also that it is invisible to its prey. It sits coiled up on a branch waiting for a bird, lizard, or tree frog to come close. Then it strikes. Like all vipers, the eyelash viper uses a powerful venom to kill its prey.

The eyelash viper (which gets its name from the little row of scales above each eye) also exists in a bright golden-yellow. This type lives in the flowers of the *Heliconia* plant. It blends in beautifully and waits for prey, such as hummingbirds, who visit the flowers for **nectar.** As they feed, the snake strikes.

Below The golden eyelash viper usually hides in brightly colored flowers for its prey.

Right This eyelash viper is colored to blend in with the moss covering of trees.

12. The rough with the smooth

One of the strongest snakes is the elephant trunk snake from Southeast Asia.This thick, heavy-bodied snake grows to a length of around 6½ ft (2 m). It has a tough, warty skin that feels very rough. This and its dull gray coloration make it look and feel just like an elephant's trunk—hence its name.

It is an almost entirely aquatic species that spends its time in warm, shallow **lagoons** and **mangrove swamps.** It is a very sluggish snake that simply sits and waits for its meal of fish to come swimming by. It is not venomous, so the fish are usually swallowed alive. Like many other types of snakes, the elephant trunk snake is hunted for its skin. The leather from this species looks very unusual because it does not have the smooth, overlapping scales of most other snakes.

In contrast to the elephant trunk snake, the green rat snake is slender and has smooth, shiny scales, which help the rat snake travel quickly over ground.

Left The green rat snake's scales look as if they are covered with oil.

Below The elephant trunk snake's skin is dry and rough.

13. Baby boom

All snakes hatch from eggs. Some species lay their eggs in a protected place, and they hatch some time later. Others hatch their eggs inside their bodies, and the female "gives birth" to live, fully-formed young. The puff adder is an example of a snake that has live young; it is special because it has so many young at one time.

Some snakes may have only two or three young; others, like the common adder, may have up to a dozen. The garter snake from North America may have twenty, thirty or even forty babies, but the puff adder has been known to have over seventy live young at one time! This is more than any other snake.

Puff adders are large, thick snakes up to 6 ½ ft (2 m) long. A pregnant female may be as thick as a human's thigh. The puff adder's fangs are enormous—over 1 in (2.5 cm) long—and they can inject powerful venom.

Young puff adders are born fully equipped with **venom sacs** and fangs, and they can kill their own prey within a week or two of being born.

Below This python has just hatched from its egg.

Right This puff adder is surrounded by a few of her new-born young.

GLOSSARY

Aquatic Living entirely or almost entirely in water. A creature such as a fish is aquatic.

Constriction Squeezing. When a snake coils its body around its prey and squeezes tightly, constriction stops the prey from breathing.

Fang A long pointed tooth. Venomous snakes have hollow fangs, which they use to inject venom into their prey.

Hood Excess skin around the neck of some snakes, such as cobras, that the snake can stretch out as a warning sign.

Lagoon A shallow salt water pond connected to the ocean.

Mangrove swamp A dense thicket of trees and shrubs growing in coastal areas.

Nectar A sugary fluid produced in flowers.

Parachute A large piece of fabric used to slow down the speed of a fall from a great height, such as from an airplane.

Pelagic A word describing creatures that live in the upper waters of the open ocean.

Predator An animal that hunts and eats other animals.

Prey Any animal that is hunted for food.

Reptile An animal, such as a snake or lizard, that has a backbone, scaly skin, and is cold-blooded.

Scent The smell of an animal. Some predators can find their prey by following its scent.

Strike A snake's attacking bite.

Tropical Of the areas just north and south of the Equator, which have very hot weather all year round.

Venomous Poisonous. A venomous snake uses venom (poisonous fluid) to kill prey.

Venom sacs The pouches filled with venom near a snake's mouth.

FURTHER READING

Discovering Snakes and Lizards, by Neil Curtis (Bookwright, 1986)
Snakes and Other Reptiles, by Mary Elting (Simon & Schuster, 1987)
Pythons and Constrictors, by Lionel Bender (Gloucester Press, 1988)
Snakes, by Ray Broekel (Children's Press, 1982)
Snakes, by Lucy Baker (Puffin, 1990)

Picture Acknowledgments

Bruce Coleman Ltd/J & D Bartlett 29, J Burton 12, C & D Firth 8, M Fogden 6, 19, 23, J Foott 10; NHPA/S Dalton 16, O Rogge 15; OSF Ltd/G I Burton 28, M Dick 4, M Fogden COVER, 22, 25, Z Leszczynski 7, 13, 14, 16, 17, 20, 21, 26, 27, D Shale 18; Planet Earth & Seaphot Ltd/K Lucas 24, R Matthews 5, C Roessler 11; Survival Anglia Ltd/M Linley 9

INDEX

Numbers in **bold** indicate photographs.